Thank You for being
A devoted husband

*From:*_____

*Date:*_____

Blessed is the man who trusts in the LORD,
whose confidence indeed is the LORD.
Jeremiah 17:7 Holman CSB

Thank You for being
A devoted husband

Thank You for being A devoted husband

Table of Contents

Introduction

Because you're reading this book, you're probably a married man. As a faithful husband, you know that caring for your family is hard work—lots of hard work. So, because of all the wonderful things you do for your wife and your family, you deserve a heartfelt "thank you," and that's exactly what this book is intended to do.

How desperately our world needs Christian men who are willing to honor God with their service. That's why our world needs husbands—like you—whose vision is clear and whose intentions are pure.

Every day provides opportunities to put God where He belongs: at the center of your thoughts and prayers. When you do so, you will worship your Creator not just with words, but also with deeds. And then, just as He promised, God will smile upon you, and upon generations yet unborn.

As you face the inevitable challenges of modern-day family life—the ups, the downs, and the complications of life here in the 21st century—you should arm yourself with the promises and principles found in God's Word. When you do, then you and your loved ones can expect the best not only for the day ahead, but also for all eternity.

To My Devoted Husband:

Thank You for

Your Love

If I speak the languages of men and of angels,
but do not have love,
I am a sounding gong or a clanging cymbal.

1 Corinthians 13:1 Holman CSB

Love is a journey. A healthy marriage is a lifelong exercise in love, fidelity, trust, understanding, forgiveness, caring, sharing, and encouragement. It requires empathy, tenderness, patience, and perseverance. It is the union of two adults, both of whom are willing to compromise and, when appropriate, to apologize. It requires heaping helpings of common sense, common courtesy, and uncommon caring. A healthy marriage—like ours—is a joy to experience and a blessing forever.

Thank you for being a faithful, loving husband. The world has taken notice of your compassion . . . and so have I.

Both a good marriage and a bad marriage have moments of struggle, but in a healthy relationship, the husband and wife search for answers and areas of agreement because they love each other.

James Dobson

There is no more lovely, friendly, and charming relationship, communion, or company than a good marriage.

Martin Luther

You should only say "I love you" on the days that end in "y".

Anonymous

A man and woman should choose each other for life for the simple reason that a long life is barely enough time for a man and woman to understand each other, and to understand is to love.

George Truett

After the forgiving comes laughter, a deeper love— and further opportunities to forgive.

Ruth Bell Graham

Love is most often found in the home—in the presence of a caring and considerate mate who nurtures love daily.

Zig Ziglar

Love simply cannot spring up without
that self-surrender to each other.
If either withholds the self,
love cannot exist.

—

E. Stanley Jones

*Life without love is
empty and meaningless
no matter how gifted we are.*

—

Charles Stanley

If you happen to be the loving spouse of a loving spouse, count yourself richly blessed.

Marie T. Freeman

Those who abandon ship the first time it enters a storm miss the calm beyond. And the rougher the storms weathered together, the deeper and stronger real love grows.

Ruth Bell Graham

Love is not grabbing, or self-centered, or selfish. Real love is being able to contribute to the happiness of another person without expecting to get anything in return.

James Dobson

We love because He first loved us.

1 John 4:19 Holman CSB

*Nevertheless let each one of you in particular
so love his own wife as himself, and let the wife see
that she respects her husband.*

Ephesians 5:33 NKJV

*Therefore shall a man leave his father and his mother,
and shall cleave unto his wife: and they shall be one flesh.*

Genesis 2:24 KJV

*So then, they are no longer two but one flesh. Therefore
what God has joined together, let not man separate.*

Matthew 19:6 NKJV

I pray that you, being rooted and firmly established in love,
may be able to comprehend with all the saints what is
the breadth and width, height and depth, and to know
the Messiah's love that surpasses knowledge, so you may be
filled with all the fullness of God.

Ephesians 3:17-19 Holman CSB

Now these three remain: faith, hope, and love.
But the greatest of these is love.

1 Corinthians 13:13 Holman CSB

Dear friends, if God loved us in this way,
we also must love one another.

1 John 4:11 Holman CSB

A HUSBAND'S PRAYER

—

*Dear Lord, You have blessed our marriage
with a love that is infinite and eternal,
and I thank You. In response to Your gifts,
Father, I will share Your love with my wife,
with my family, with my friends,
and with the world today and every day.*

Amen

To My Devoted Husband:

Thank You for Listening

A wise man will listen and increase his learning,
and a discerning man will obtain guidance.

Proverbs 1:5 Holman CSB

Thanks for listening . . . and for understanding. We live in a busy world, a place where it is all too easy to take our loved ones for granted, but you never did that. You could have placed other priorities above our marriage, but you refused to do so. Instead, you invested time and energy in our marriage. God bless you.

Listening is loving.

Zig Ziglar

The cliché is true: People don't care what we know until they know we care.

Rick Warren

The first service one owes to others in the fellowship consists in listening to them. Just as love of God begins in listening to His Word, so the beginning of love for the brethren is learning to listen to them. It is God's love for us that He not only gives us His Word but lends us His ear. So it is His work that we do for our brother when we learn to listen to him.

Dietrich Bonhoeffer

One of the best ways to encourage someone who's hurting is with your ears—by listening.

Barbara Johnson

In the soul-searching of our lives, we are to stay quiet so we can hear Him say all that He wants to say to us in our hearts.

Charles Swindoll

We cannot experience the fullness of Christ if we do all the expressing. We must allow God to express His love, will, and truth to us.

Gary Smalley

When we come to Jesus stripped of pretensions, with a needy spirit, ready to listen, He meets us at the point of need.

Catherine Marshall

The fewer words, the better prayer.

Martin Luther

Part of good communication is listening with the eyes
as well as with the ears.

Josh McDowell

Attitude and the spirit in which we communicate
are as important as the words we say.

Charles Stanley

We should ask ourselves three things before we speak:
Is it true? Is it kind? Does it glorify God?

Billy Graham

He awakens [Me] each morning; He awakens My ear to listen like those being instructed. The Lord GOD has opened My ear, and I was not rebellious; I did not turn back.

Isaiah 50:4-5 Holman CSB

You must follow the LORD your God and fear Him. You must keep His commands and listen to His voice; you must worship Him and remain faithful to Him.

Deuteronomy 13:4 Holman CSB

The one who is from God listens to God's words. This is why you don't listen, because you are not from God.

John 8:47 Holman CSB

My dearly loved brothers, understand this:
everyone must be quick to hear, slow to speak, and slow to anger.

James 1:19 Holman CSB

A fool's way is right in his own eyes,
but whoever listens to counsel is wise.

Proverbs 12:15 Holman CSB

Listen to counsel and receive instruction so that
you may be wise in later life.

Proverbs 19:20 Holman CSB

A HUSBAND'S PRAYER

—

Dear Lord, make me a careful listener.
When I listen, I learn. So, today and every day,
I will strive to understand my wife, my family, my
friends, and my world as I follow
in the footsteps of Your Son.
Amen

To My Devoted Husband:

Thank You for
Wise Decisions

Acquire wisdom—how much better it is than gold!
And acquire understanding—it is preferable to silver:

Proverbs 16:16 Holman CSB

One of life's great ironies is that there is so much to learn and so little time. That's why we value the lessons you have taught us and the ones that we still have to learn.

Wisdom is not like a mushroom; it does not spring up overnight. It is, instead, like an oak tree that starts as a tiny acorn, grows into a sapling, and eventually reaches up to the sky, tall and strong. To become wise, we must seek God's wisdom and live according to His Word. And, we must not only learn the lessons of the Christian life; we must also live by them. And you've done that.

Thanks for sharing your wisdom . . . we need it more now than ever.

Most of us go through life praying a little, planning a little, jockeying for position, hoping but never being quite certain of anything, and always secretly afraid that we will miss the way. This is a tragic waste of truth and never gives rest to the heart. There is a better way. It is to repudiate our own wisdom and take instead the infinite wisdom of God.

A. W. Tozer

The first thing we have to do to receive God's guidance is to reevaluate our current guidance systems.

Bill Hybels

Knowledge is horizontal. Wisdom is vertical; it comes down from above.

Billy Graham

There is a difficulty about disagreeing with God. He is the source from which all your reasoning power comes: you could not be right and He wrong any more than a stream can rise higher than its own source. When you are arguing against Him you are arguing against the very power that makes you able to argue at all: it is like cutting off the branch you are sitting on.

C. S. Lewis

Do you want to be wise? Choose wise friends.

Charles Swindoll

The doorstep to the temple of wisdom is a knowledge of our own ignorance.

C. H. Spurgeon

The fruit of wisdom is Christlikeness, peace, humility, and love. And, the root of it is faith in Christ as the manifested wisdom of God.

J. I. Packer

The more wisdom enters our hearts, the more we will be able to trust our hearts in difficult situations.

John Eldredge

The man who prays ceases to be a fool.

Oswald Chambers

Let your old age be childlike, and childhood like old age;
that is, so that neither may your wisdom be with pride,
nor your humility without wisdom.

St. Augustine

The essence of wisdom, from a practical standpoint,
is pausing long enough to look at our lives—invitations,
opportunities, relationships—from God's perspective.
And then acting on it.

Charles Stanley

If you lack knowledge, go to school.
If you lack wisdom,
get on your knees.

—

Vance Havner

So teach us to number our days, that we may gain a heart of wisdom.

Psalm 90:12 NKJV

Those who are wise will shine like the bright expanse [of the heavens], and those who lead many to righteousness, like the stars forever and ever.

Daniel 12:3 Holman CSB

But from Him you are in Christ Jesus, who for us became wisdom from God, as well as righteousness, sanctification, and redemption.

1 Corinthians 1:30 Holman CSB

The fear of the LORD is the beginning of wisdom;
a good understanding have all those who do
His commandments. His praise endures forever.

Psalm 111:10 NKJV

Therefore, everyone who hears these words of Mine and acts
on them will be like a sensible man who built his house on
the rock. The rain fell, the rivers rose, and the winds blew and
pounded that house. Yet it didn't collapse,
because its foundation was on the rock.

Matthew 7:24–25 Holman CSB

A wise man will hear and increase learning,
and a man of understanding will attain wise counsel.

Proverbs 1:5 NKJV

A HUSBAND'S PRAYER

—

*Dear Lord, when I trust in the wisdom of
the world, I am often led astray, but when
I trust in Your wisdom, I build my life upon
a firm foundation. Today and every day
I will strive to be a man who trusts Your Word
and follows it, knowing that the ultimate
wisdom is Your wisdom and
the ultimate truth is Your truth.*

Amen

To My Devoted Husband:

Thank You for Your Positive Attitude

Finally brothers, whatever is true, whatever is honorable,
whatever is just, whatever is pure, whatever is lovely,
whatever is commendable—if there is any moral excellence
and if there is any praise—dwell on these things.

Philippians 4:8 Holman CSB

The Christian life is a cause for celebration, but sometimes we don't feel much like celebrating. In fact, when the weight of the world seems to bear down upon our shoulders, celebration may be the last thing on our minds . . . but it shouldn't be. As God's children, we are all blessed beyond measure on good days and bad.

Thanks for your positive attitude. Thanks for thinking optimistically about yourself, about your future, and about our marriage—your attitude is a blessing to both of us.

———

Life is 10% what happens to you
and 90% how you respond to it.

Charles Swindoll

The essence of optimism is that it takes no account of the present, but it is a source of inspiration, of vitality, and of hope. Where others have resigned, it enables a man to hold his head high, to claim the future for himself, and not abandon it to his enemy.

Dietrich Bonhoeffer

The people whom I have seen succeed best in life have always been cheerful and hopeful people who went about their business with a smile on their faces.

Charles Kingsley

If our hearts have been attuned to God through an abiding faith in Christ, the result will be joyous optimism and good cheer.

Billy Graham

It is a remarkable thing that some of the most optimistic and enthusiastic people you will meet are those who have been through intense suffering.

Warren Wiersbe

The popular idea of faith is of a certain obstinate optimism: the hope, tenaciously held in the face of trouble, that the universe is fundamentally friendly and things may get better.

J. I. Packer

Keep your feet on the ground, but let your heart soar as high as it will. Refuse to be average or to surrender to the chill of your spiritual environment.

A. W. Tozer

When you believe that nothing significant can happen through you, you have said more about your belief in God than you have said about yourself.

Henry Blackaby

Great leaders understand that the right attitude will set the right atmosphere, which enables the right response from others.

John Maxwell

You've heard the saying, "Life is what you make it." That means we have a choice. We can choose to have a life full of frustration and fear, but we can just as easily choose one of joy and contentment.

Dennis Swanberg

For the word of God is living and powerful, and sharper
than any two-edged sword, piercing even to the division
of soul and spirit, and of joints and marrow,
and is a discerner of the thoughts and intents of the heart.

Hebrews 4:12 NKJV

A cheerful heart has a continual feast.

Proverbs 15:15 Holman CSB

Let your eyes look forward; fix your gaze straight ahead.

Proverbs 4:25 Holman CSB

Make me hear joy and gladness.

Psalm 51:8 NKJV

Make your own attitude that of Christ Jesus.

Philippians 2:5 Holman CSB

Set your minds on what is above, not on what is on the earth.

Colossians 3:2 Holman CSB

*Let this mind be in you which was also in Christ Jesus,
who, being in the form of God, did not consider it robbery
to be equal with God, but made Himself of no reputation,
taking the form of a bondservant, and coming in the likeness
of men. And being found in appearance as a man,
He humbled Himself and became obedient to the point
of death, even the death of the cross.*

Philippians 2:5-8 NKJV

A HUSBAND'S PRAYER

—

Lord, let me be an expectant Christian.
Let me expect the best from You, and let me look
for the best in others. If I become discouraged,
Father, turn my thoughts and my prayers to You.
Let me trust You, Lord, to direct my life.
And, let me be Your faithful, hopeful,
optimistic servant every day that I live.
Amen

To My Devoted Husband:

Thank You for

Your Godly

Lifestyle

Sow righteousness for yourselves and reap faithful love;
break up your untilled ground. It is time to seek the LORD
until He comes and sends righteousness on you like the rain.

Hosea 10:12 Holman CSB

L ife is a series of choices—thanks for making good ones. When we live according to God's commandments, we earn for ourselves the abundance and peace that He intends for us to experience. When we obey God's Holy Word, we are blessed. And because of your wise choices, you have blessed our marriage, our family, and our home.

Righteousness not only defines God,
but God defines righteousness.

Bill Hybels

It may be said without qualification that every man is as holy and as full of the Spirit as he wants to be. He may not be as full as he wishes he were, but he is most certainly as full as he wants to be.

A. W. Tozer

Have your heart right with Christ, and he will visit you often, and so turn weekdays into Sundays, meals into sacraments, homes into temples, and earth into heaven.

C. H. Spurgeon

The great thing is to be found at one's post as a child of God, living each day as though it were our last, but planning as though our world might last a hundred years.

C. S. Lewis

What is God looking for? He is looking for men and women whose hearts are completely His.

Charles Swindoll

A life growing in its purity and devotion will be a more prayerful life.

E. M. Bounds

If we don't hunger and thirst after righteousness, we'll become anemic and feel miserable in our Christian experience.

Franklin Graham

We must appropriate the tender mercy of God every day after conversion, or problems quickly develop. We need his grace daily in order to live a righteous life.

Jim Cymbala

It is quite true to say, "I can't live a holy life," but you can decide to let Jesus make you holy.

Oswald Chambers

Learning God's truth and getting it into our heads is one thing, but living God's truth and getting it into our characters is quite something else.

Warren Wiersbe

The righteous one will live by his faith.

Habakkuk 2:4 Holman CSB

And the world is passing away, and the lust of it; but he who does the will of God abides forever.

1 John 2:17 NKJV

Because the eyes of the Lord are on the righteous and His ears are open to their request. But the face of the Lord is against those who do evil.

1 Peter 3:12 Holman CSB

Flee from youthful passions, and pursue righteousness, faith, love, and peace, along with those who call on the Lord from a pure heart.

2 Timothy 2:22 Holman CSB

Therefore, come out from among them and be separate,
says the Lord; do not touch any unclean thing,
and I will welcome you.

2 Corinthians 6:17 Holman CSB

And now, Israel, what does the LORD your God ask of you
except to fear the LORD your God by walking in all His ways,
to love Him, and to worship the LORD your God
with all your heart and all your soul?

Deuteronomy 10:12 Holman CSB

Do what is right and good in the LORD's sight, so that you may
prosper and so that you may enter and possess the good land
the LORD your God swore to [give] your fathers.

Deuteronomy 6:18 Holman CSB

A HUSBAND'S PRAYER

—

Lord, this world is filled with temptations, distractions, and frustrations. When I turn my thoughts away from You and Your Word, I suffer. But when I trust in Your commandments, when I turn my thoughts, my faith, and my prayers to You, I am safe. Direct my path far from the temptations and distractions of the world. Let me discover Your will and follow it, Father, this day and always.

Amen

To My Devoted Husband:

Thank You for Your Commitment to Our Church

Be on guard for yourselves and for all the flock, among whom the Holy Spirit has appointed you as overseers, to shepherd the church of God, which He purchased with His own blood.

Acts 20:28 Holman CSB

I n the Book of Acts, Luke reminds us to "feed the church of God" (20:28). As Christians who have been saved by a loving, compassionate Creator, we are compelled not only to worship Him in our hearts but also to worship Him in the presence of fellow believers.

Thanks for your commitment to the church. What a difference it has made in our lives.

—

The empty tomb proves Christianity.
The empty church denies it.

Anonymous

The New Testament does not envisage solitary religion; some kind of regular assembly for worship and instruction is everywhere taken for granted in the epistles.

C. S. Lewis

We are hearing today about those who like Christ but do no like the church. But Christ loved the church and gave Himself for it. How can we like the Head but not the Body, the Groom but not the Bride?

Vance Havner

Only participation in the full life of a local church builds spiritual muscle.

Rick Warren

The church needs people who are doers of the Word and not just hearers.

Warren Wiersbe

Nothing under the sun can be as dry and flat and tedious and exhausting as "church work" without the Spirit.

Vance Havner

The Bible knows nothing of solitary religion.

John Wesley

Christians have spent their whole lives mastering all sorts of principles, done their duty, carried on the programs of their church . . . and never known God intimately, heart to heart.

John Eldredge

The church is where it's at. The first place of Christian service
for any Christian is in a local church.

Jerry Clower

What the church needs is not better machinery nor new
organizations, but instead it needs men whom
the Holy Spirit can use—men of prayer,
men mighty in prayer.

E. M. Bounds

To model the kingdom of God in the world, the church must
not only be a repentant community, committed to truth,
but also a holy community.

Chuck Colson

For we are God's fellow workers; you are God's field,
you are God's building.

1 Corinthians 3:9 NKJV

And let us be concerned about one another in order
to promote love and good works.

Hebrews 10:24 Holman CSB

And I also say to you that you are Peter, and on this rock I will
build My church, and the forces of Hades will not overpower it.
I will give you the keys of the kingdom of heaven, and whatever
you bind on earth will have been bound in heaven, and
whatever you loose on earth will have been loosed in heaven.

Matthew 16:18-19 Holman CSB

For where two or three are gathered together in My name,

I am there among them.

Matthew 18:20 Holman CSB

Now you are the body of Christ, and individual members of it.

I Corinthians 12:27 Holman CSB

Do not be unequally yoked together with unbelievers.
For what fellowship has righteousness with lawlessness?
And what communion has light with darkness?

2 Corinthians 6:14 NKJV

A HUSBAND'S PRAYER

—

*Dear Lord, I thank You for Your church . . .
and for what Your church means to my family.
When we worship together, I realize how
richly we have been blessed. Let my family's
participation in the church demonstrate the love
we feel for each other and the love we feel for You.*

Amen

To My Devoted Husband:

Thank You for
Your Humility
and Strength

He has told you men what is good and what it is
the LORD requires of you: Only to act justly, to love faithfulness,
and to walk humbly with your God.

Micah 6:8 Holman CSB

Sometimes, it's easy to puff out our chests and proclaim, "I did that!" But you have not allowed pride to be your downfall.

God honors men (like you) who become humble servants; men who care less for their own glory and more for God's glory.

There is no such thing as a self-made man. All men are made by God . . . and He deserves the glory—thanks for giving it to Him.

—

The great characteristic of the saint is humility.

Oswald Chambers

You can see the world standing tall,
but to witness the Savior, you have to get on your knees.

Max Lucado

Seeking after God is a two-pronged endeavor.
It requires not only humility to say, "God, I need you,"
but also a heart that desires a pure life that is
pleasing to the Lord.

Jim Cymbala

The preoccupation with self is the enemy of humility.

Franklin Graham

It is very easy to overestimate the importance of our own achievements in comparison with what we owe others.

Dietrich Bonhoeffer

Humility is the fairest and rarest flower that blooms.

Charles Swindoll

Humility expresses a genuine dependency on God and others.

Charles Stanley

One never can see, or not till long afterwards, why any one was selected for any job. And when one does, it is usually some reason that leaves no room for vanity.

C. S. Lewis

Let the love of Christ be believed in and felt in your hearts, and it will humble you.

C. H. Spurgeon

Jesus had a humble heart. If He abides in us, pride will never dominate our lives.

Billy Graham

I can usually sense that a leading is from the Holy Spirit when it calls me to humble myself, to serve somebody, to encourage somebody, or to give something away. Very rarely will the evil one lead us to do those kind of things.

Bill Hybels

If My people who are called by My name will humble themselves, and pray and seek My face, and turn from their wicked ways, then I will hear from heaven, and will forgive their sin and heal their land.

2 Chronicles 7:14 NKJV

Do nothing out of rivalry or conceit, but in humility consider others as more important than yourselves.

Philippians 2:3 Holman CSB

"I assure you," He said, "unless you are converted and become like children, you will never enter the kingdom of heaven. Therefore, whoever humbles himself like this child— this one is the greatest in the kingdom of heaven."

Matthew 18:3-4 Holman CSB

Clothe yourselves with humility toward one another, because
God resists the proud, but gives grace to the humble.

1 Peter 5:5 Holman CSB

Humble yourselves therefore under the mighty hand of God,
so that He may exalt you in due time, casting all your care
upon Him, because He cares about you.

1 Peter 5:6-7 Holman CSB

But He said to me, "My grace is sufficient for you, for power is
perfected in weakness." Therefore, I will most gladly boast
all the more about my weaknesses, so that
Christ's power may reside in me.

2 Corinthians 12:9 Holman CSB

A HUSBAND'S PRAYER

—

Lord, make me a man with a humble heart.
Keep me mindful, Dear God, that all my gifts
come from You. When I feel prideful,
remind me that You sent Your Son to be
a humble carpenter and that Jesus was ridiculed
on a cross. Let me grow beyond my need
for earthly praise, Lord, and when
I seek approval, let me look only to You.

Amen

To My Devoted Husband:

Thank You for Your Enthusiasm

*Whatever you do, do it enthusiastically,
as something done for the Lord and not for men.*
Colossians 3:23 Holman CSB

A husband's attitude affects the entire family, and your enthusiasm is contagious. Because you are upbeat and enthusiastic, we can be, too.

Thanks for listening to our dreams—and thanks for believing in them. When we summoned the courage to confide in you, you supported us, you encouraged us, and you trusted us. If you harbored any doubts, you hid them.

Your optimism gives us the courage to keep dreaming... and the faith to believe that our dreams can come true.

—

Enthusiasm, like the flu, is contagious—
we get it from one another.

Barbara Johnson

There seems to be a chilling fear of holy enthusiasm among the people of God. We try to tell how happy we are—but we remain so well-controlled that there are very few waves of glory experienced in our midst.

A. W. Tozer

One of the great needs in the church today is for every Christian to become enthusiastic about his faith in Jesus Christ.

Billy Graham

We act as though comfort and luxury were the chief requirements of life, when all we need to make us really happy is something to be enthusiastic about.

Charles Kingsley

God commands us to be filled with the Spirit, and if we are not filled, it is because we are living beneath our privileges.

D. L. Moody

Prayer must be aflame. Prayer without fervor is as a sun without light or heat, or as a flower without beauty or fragrance. A soul devoted to God is a fervent soul, and prayer is the creature of that flame. He only can truly pray who is all aglow for holiness, for God, and for heaven.

E. M. Bounds

Don't take hold of a thing unless you want that thing to take hold of you.

E. Stanley Jones

Wherever you are, be all there. Live to the hilt
every situation you believe to be the will of God.

Jim Elliot

When we wholeheartedly commit ourselves to God,
there is nothing mediocre or run-of-the-mill about us.
To live for Christ is to be passionate about
our Lord and about our lives.

Jim Gallery

Catch on fire with enthusiasm and people will come
for miles to watch you burn.

John Wesley

I have seen that there is nothing better than for a person to enjoy his activities, because that is his reward. For who can enable him to see what will happen after he dies?

Ecclesiastes 3:22 Holman CSB

He did it with all his heart. So be prospered.

2 Chronicles 31:21 NKJV

Do not lack diligence; be fervent in spirit; serve the Lord.

Romans 12:11 Holman CSB

Rejoice in the Lord always. I will say it again: Rejoice!

Philippians 4:4 Holman CSB

Be strong and courageous, and do the work. Don't be afraid or discouraged, for the LORD God, my God, is with you. He won't leave you or forsake you.

1 Chronicles 28:20 Holman CSB

I have spoken these things to you so that My joy may be in you and your joy may be complete.

John 15:11 Holman CSB

Delight yourself also in the LORD, and He shall give you the desires of your heart.

Psalm 37:4 NKJV

A HUSBAND'S PRAYER

—

Dear Lord, You have called me not to a life of mediocrity, but to a life of passion. Today, I will celebrate my life and my family as I follow Your Son. I will share Christ's Good News—and His love— with all who cross my path.

Amen

To My Devoted Husband:

Thank You for Your Time

There is an occasion for everything,
and a time for every activity under heaven.

Ecclesiastes 3:1 Holman CSB

You have never been too busy for our family, and you've never been too busy for me. Thanks for your time. Whatever we did and wherever we did it, you were right there in our corner, cheering us on—and we noticed.

As you know all too well, time is a precious thing, a priceless treasure that should never be squandered. You have valued our time together . . . and that has made all the difference.

—

Our time is short! The time we can invest for God, in creative things, in receiving our fellowmen for Christ, is short!

Billy Graham

As we surrender the use of our time to the lordship of Christ, He will lead us to use it in the most productive way imaginable.

Charles Stanley

Time here on earth is limited . . . use it or lose it!

Jim Gallery

The more time you give to something, the more you reveal its importance and value to you.

Rick Warren

Our leisure, even our play, is a matter of serious concern. There is no neutral ground in the universe: every square inch, every split second, is claimed by God and counterclaimed by Satan.

C. S. Lewis

Frustration is not the will of God. There is time to do anything and everything that God wants us to do.

Elisabeth Elliot

Having values keeps a person focused on the important things.

John Maxwell

God has a present will for your life. It is neither chaotic nor utterly exhausting. In the midst of many good choices vying for your time, He will give you the discernment to recognize what is best.

Beth Moore

The best use of life is love. The best expression of love is time. The best time to love is now.

Rick Warren

Overcommitment and time pressures are the greatest destroyers of marriages and families. It takes time to develop any friendship, whether with a loved one or with God himself.

James Dobson

Come to Me, all you who are weary and burdened, and I will give you rest. Take My yoke upon you and learn from Me, because I am gentle and humble in heart, and you will find rest for your souls. For My yoke is easy and My burden is light.

Matthew 11:28–30 Holman CSB

Therefore the LORD is waiting to show you mercy, and is rising up to show you compassion, for the LORD is a just God. Happy are all who wait patiently for Him.

Isaiah 30:18 Holman CSB

Dear friends, don't let this one thing escape you: with the Lord one day is like 1,000 years, and 1,000 years like one day.

2 Peter 3:8 Holman CSB

He has made everything appropriate in its time. He has also put eternity in their hearts, but man cannot discover the work God has done from beginning to end.

Ecclesiastes 3:11 Holman CSB

But seek first the kingdom of God and His righteousness, and all these things will be provided for you.

Matthew 6:33 Holman CSB

So teach us to number our days, that we may gain a heart of wisdom.

Psalm 90:12 NKJV

And the world with its lust is passing away, but the one who does God's will remains forever.

1 John 2:17 Holman CSB

A HUSBAND'S PRAYER

—

Lord, let Your priorities be my priorities.
Let Your will be my will. Let Your Word
be my guide, and let me grow in faith
and in wisdom this day and every day.

Amen

To My Devoted Husband:

Thank You for
Sharing God's
Peace

I have told you these things so that in Me you may have peace.
In the world you have suffering.
But take courage! I have conquered the world.

John 16:33 Holman CSB

The beautiful words of John 14:27 give us hope: "Peace I leave with you, my peace I give unto you . . ." Jesus offers us peace, not as the world gives, but as He alone gives. We, as believers, can accept His peace or ignore it.

When we accept the peace of Jesus Christ into our hearts, our lives are transformed. And then, because we possess the gift of peace, we can share that gift with others.

You have shared God's peace with me, with our family, and with the world. Bless you.

Beth Moore

Prayer guards hearts and minds and causes God
to bring peace out of chaos.

When we do what is right, we have contentment, peace, and happiness.

Beverly LaHaye

Christ alone can bring lasting peace—peace with God—peace among men and nations—and peace within our hearts.

Billy Graham

The more closely you cling to the Lord Jesus, the more clear will your peace be.

C. H. Spurgeon

To know God as He really is—in His essential nature and character—is to arrive at a citadel of peace that circumstances may storm, but can never capture.

Catherine Marshall

Look around you and you'll be distressed;
look within yourself and you'll be depressed;
look at Jesus, and you'll be at rest!

Corrie ten Boom

We must learn to move according to the timetable
of the Timeless One, and to be at peace.

Elisabeth Elliot

There may be no trumpet sound or loud applause
when we make a right decision, just a calm sense of
resolution and peace.

Gloria Gaither

Where the soul is full of peace and joy, outward surroundings and circumstances are of comparatively little account.

Hannah Whitall Smith

The Bible instructs—and experience teaches— that praising God results in our burdens being lifted and our joys being multiplied.

Jim Gallery

God is in control of history; it's His story. Doesn't that give you a great peace—especially when world events seem so tumultuous and insane?

Kay Arthur

God has called us to peace.

1 Corinthians 7:15 NKJV

Be of good comfort, be of one mind, live in peace;
and the God of love and peace will be with you.

2 Corinthians 13:11 NKJV

The result of righteousness will be peace;
the effect of righteousness will be quiet confidence forever.

Isaiah 32:17 Holman CSB

Abundant peace belongs to those who love Your instruction; nothing makes them stumble.

Psalm 119:165 Holman CSB

For He is our peace.

Ephesians 2:14 Holman CSB

Return unto thy rest, O my soul; for the LORD hath dealt bountifully with thee.

Psalm 116:7 KJV

A HUSBAND'S PRAYER

—

The world talks about peace, but only You,
Lord, can give a perfect and lasting peace.
True peace comes through the Prince of Peace,
and sometimes His peace passes
all understanding. Help me to accept
His peace—and share it—
this day and forever.
Amen

To My Devoted Husband:

Thank You for

Praising and

Worshipping God

Praise the LORD! Oh, give thanks to the LORD, for He is good!

For His mercy endures forever.

Psalm 106:1 NKJV

The Bible teaches that we should worship God in our hearts and in our churches—you've done both, and your family thanks you.

We live in a world teeming with temptations and distractions—a world where good and evil struggle in a constant battle to win our minds, our hearts, and our souls. Thank you for choosing to worship God, and for teaching us to do the same.

—

When there is peace in the heart,
there will be praise on the lips.

Warren Wiersbe

When we come before the Lord with praise, humbly repent of our transgressions, and in obedience present our petitions to God according to the guidelines set out for us in Scripture, He will answer.

Shirley Dobson

Praise opens the window of our hearts, preparing us to walk more closely with God. Prayer raises the window of our spirit, enabling us to listen more clearly to the Father.

Max Lucado

Two wings are necessary to lift our souls toward God: prayer and praise. Prayer asks. Praise accepts the answer.

Mrs. Charles E. Cowman

Be not afraid of saying too much in the praises of God;
all the danger is of saying too little.

Matthew Henry

What happens when we praise the Father?
We reestablish the proper chain of command.

Max Lucado

The Bible instructs—and experience teaches—
that praising God results in our burdens being lifted
and our joys being multiplied.

Jim Gallery

How delightful a teacher, but gentle a provider,
how bountiful a giver is my Father!
Praise, praise to Thee, O manifested Most High.

Jim Elliot

Worship is an act which develops feelings for God,
not a feeling for God which is expressed in an act of
worship. When we obey the command to praise God
in worship, our deep, essential need to be in
relationship with God is nurtured.

Eugene Peterson

Most of the verses written about praise in God's Word were
voiced by people faced with crushing heartaches, injustice,
treachery, slander, and scores of other difficult situations.

Joni Eareckson Tada

From the rising of the sun to its going down
the LORD's name is to be praised.

Psalm 113:3 NKJV

Enter into His gates with thanksgiving, and into His courts
with praise. Be thankful to Him, and bless His name.
For the LORD is good; His mercy is everlasting,
and His truth endures to all generations.

Psalm 100:4-5 NKJV

So that at the name of Jesus every knee should bow—
of those who are in heaven and on earth and under the earth—
and every tongue should confess that Jesus Christ is Lord,
to the glory of God the Father.

Philippians 2:10-11 Holman CSB

But I will hope continually, and will praise You
yet more and more.

Psalm 71:14 NKJV

In everything give thanks; for this is the will of
God in Christ Jesus for you.

2 Thessalonians 5:18 NKJV

Therefore, through Him let us continually offer up to God
a sacrifice of praise, that is, the fruit of our lips
that confess His name.

Hebrews 13:15 Holman CSB

Sing to the LORD, all the earth; Proclaim the good news
of His salvation from day to day.

1 Chronicles 16:23 NKJV

A HUSBAND'S PRAYER

—

Dear Lord, make me a man who gives constant praise to You. And, let me share the joyous news of Jesus Christ with a world that needs His transformation and His salvation.

Amen

To My Devoted Husband:

Thank You for Your Leadership

Shepherd God's flock among you, not overseeing out of compulsion but freely, according to God's will; not for the money but eagerly.

1 Peter 5:2 Holman CSB

As the leader of your family, you have a profound responsibility to your loved ones and to your God. Thanks for being the kind of leader we can genuinely admire.

When someone in our family needs encouragement, you are always there. And when we need "straight talk," you are always honest and always concerned.

You strike a proper balance between discipline and fun, something which, by the way, isn't easy. But you have made it look easy . . . and we have noticed.

———

You can never separate a leader's actions from his character.

John Maxwell

True leaders are not afraid to surround themselves with people of ability—and not afraid to give those people opportunities for greatness.

Warren Wiersbe

What do we Christians chiefly value in our leaders? The answer seems to be not their holiness, but their gifts and skills and resources. The thought that only holy people are likely to be spiritually useful does not loom large in our minds.

J. I. Packer

No one deserves the right to lead without first persevering through pain and heartache and failure.

Charles Swindoll

Integrity and maturity are two character traits vital to the heart of a leader.

Charles Stanley

A true and safe leader is likely to be one who has no desire to lead, but is forced into a position of leadership by inward pressure of the Holy Spirit and the press of external situation.

A. W. Tozer

Leaders must learn how to wait. Often their followers don't always see as far as they see or have the faith that they have.

Warren Wiersbe

Great leaders understand that the right attitude will
set the right atmosphere, which enables
the right response from others.

John Maxwell

A wise leader chooses a variety of gifted individuals.
He complements his strengths.

Charles Stanley

It is amazing what will happen in your leadership when
you do not gauge the happiness of your life or
the greatness of your day by how easy it was.

John Maxwell

So then, we must pursue what promotes peace
and what builds up one another.

Romans 14:19 Holman CSB

According to the grace given to us, we have different gifts:
If prophecy, use it according to the standard of faith;
if service, in service; if teaching, in teaching; if exhorting,
in exhortation; giving, with generosity; leading, with diligence;
showing mercy, with cheerfulness.

Romans 12:6-8 Holman CSB

The Lord has found a man loyal to Him,
and the Lord has appointed him as ruler over His people.

1 Samuel 13:14 Holman CSB

His master said to him, "Well done, good and faithful slave!
You were faithful over a few things; I will put you in charge
of many things. Enter your master's joy!"

Matthew 25:21 Holman CSB

An overseer, therefore, must be above reproach, the husband
of one wife, self-controlled, sensible, respectable, hospitable,
an able teacher; not addicted to wine, not a bully
but gentle, not quarrelsome, not greedy.

1 Timothy 3:2-3 Holman CSB

And we exhort you, brothers: warn those who are lazy, comfort
the discouraged, help the weak, be patient with everyone.

1 Thessalonians 5:14 Holman CSB

A HUSBAND'S PRAYER

—

Dear Lord, when I find myself in a position of leadership, let me seek Your will and obey Your commandments. Make me a man of integrity and wisdom, Lord, and make me a worthy example to those whom I serve.

Let me be a Christ-centered leader, and let me turn to You, Father, for guidance, for courage, for wisdom, and for love.

Amen

To My Devoted Husband:
Thank You for
Trusting God

Trust in the LORD with all your heart, and do not rely
on your own understanding; think about Him in all your ways,
and He will guide you on the right paths.

Proverbs 3:5-6 Holman CSB

I t's easy to talk about trusting God, but actually trusting Him day by day is considerably harder. Why? Because genuinely trusting God requires more than words; it requires a willingness to follow God's lead and a willingness to obey His commandments.

Thank you for trusting God. He has never let you down, and He never will. You know that God can handle your troubles infinitely better than you can . . . thanks for letting Him do it.

God's omniscience can instill you with a supernatural
confidence that can transform your life.

Bill Hybels

Attitude is all-important. Let the soul take a quiet attitude of faith and love toward God, and from there on, the responsibility is God's. He will make good on His commitments.

A. W. Tozer

Our only means of living in Him is by faith, so trusting Him to see us through any and all trials and testings delights our Lord!

Bill Bright

It is a dreadful truth that the state of having to depend solely on God is what we all dread most . . . . It is good of Him to force us, but dear me, how hard to feel that it is good at the time.

C. S. Lewis

As we trust Him, God helps us endure and even discern His purposes in the midst of suffering.

Billy Graham

It is one thing to love the ways of the Lord when all is well and quite another thing to cling to them during discouragement or difficulty.

C. H. Spurgeon

Fear lurks in the shadows of every area of life. The future may look very threatening. Jesus says, "Stop being afraid. Trust me!"

Charles Swindoll

Trust in yourself and you are doomed to disappointment; trust in money and you may have it taken from you, but trust in God, and you are never to be confounded in time or eternity.

D. L. Moody

Mary could not have dreamed all that would result from her faithful obedience. Likewise, you cannot possibly imagine all that God has in store for you when you trust him.

Henry Blackaby

There is no other method of living piously and justly than that of depending upon God.

John Calvin

Let us hold fast the confession of our hope without wavering,
for He who promised is faithful.

Hebrews 10:23 NKJV

For we walk by faith, not by sight.

2 Corinthians 5:7 NKJV

The one who understands a matter finds success,
and the one who trusts in the LORD will be happy.

Proverbs 16:20 Holman CSB

For the eyes of the LORD range throughout the earth to show
Himself strong for those whose hearts are completely His.

2 Chronicles 16:9 Holman CSB

He granted their request because they trusted in Him.

1 Chronicles 5:20 Holman CSB

LORD, I turn my hope to You. My God, I trust in You.
Do not let me be disgraced;
do not let my enemies gloat over me.

Psalm 25:1-2 Holman CSB

The fear of man is a snare, but the one who trusts
in the LORD is protected.

Proverbs 29:25 Holman CSB

A HUSBAND'S PRAYER

—

Dear Lord, sometimes I face challenges that leave me worried and afraid. When I am fearful, let me seek Your strength. When I am anxious, give me faith. Keep me mindful, Lord, that You are my God. With You by my side, Lord, I have nothing to fear today, tomorrow, or forever.

Amen

To My Devoted Husband:

Thank You for Your Example

You should be an example to the believers in speech, in conduct, in love, in faith, in purity.

1 Timothy 4:12 Holman CSB

Every family (including ours) needs positive role models. Thanks for being one. You have taught us some of life's most important lessons, not only by your words but also by your actions.

You weren't always perfect—nobody is—but when you made mistakes, you corrected them, you moved on, and we learned.

Because of the example you've set, you are a powerful force for good inside our home . . . and far beyond.

———

Living life with a consistent spiritual walk
deeply influences those we love most.

Vonette Bright

There is too much sermonizing and too little witnessing.
People do not come to Christ at the end of an argument.

Vance Havner

For one man who can introduce another to Jesus Christ
by the way he lives and by the atmosphere of his life,
there are a thousand who can only talk jargon about him.

Oswald Chambers

In our faith we leave footprints to guide others.
A child, a friend, a recent convert.
None should be left to walk the trail alone.

Max Lucado

Among the most joyful people I have known have been some who seem to have had no human reason for joy. The sweet fragrance of Christ has shown through their lives.

Elisabeth Elliot

The religion of Jesus Christ has an ethical as well as a doctrinal side.

Lottie Moon

Your life will not convince those around you of the reality of Jesus if you cannot live in unity with your fellow Christians.

Henry Blackaby

Your life is destined to be an example.
The only question is "what kind?"

—

Marie T. Freeman

Each one of us is God's special work of art. Through us, He teaches and inspires, delights and encourages, informs and uplifts all those who view our lives. God, the master artist, is most concerned about expressing Himself—His thoughts and His intentions—through what He paints in our character . . . . [He] wants to paint a beautiful portrait of His Son in and through your life.

A painting like no other in all of time.

Joni Eareckson Tada

We urgently need people who encourage and inspire us to move toward God and away from the world's enticing pleasures.

Jim Cymbala

Our walk counts far more than our talk, always!

—

George Mueller

*Do everything without grumbling and arguing,
so that you may be blameless and pure.*

Philippians 2:14–15 Holman CSB

*Set an example of good works yourself,
with integrity and dignity in your teaching.*

Titus 2:7 Holman CSB

For the kingdom of God is not in talk but in power:

1 Corinthians 4:20 Holman CSB

*Therefore since we also have such a large cloud of witnesses
surrounding us, let us lay aside every weight
and the sin that so easily ensnares us, and run
with endurance the race that lies before us.*

Hebrews 12:1 Holman CSB

I, therefore, the prisoner in the Lord, urge you to walk worthy of the calling you have received.

Ephesians 4:1 Holman CSB

But whoever keeps His word, truly in him the love of God is perfected. This is how we know we are in Him: the one who says he remains in Him should walk just as He walked.

1 John 2:5-6 Holman CSB

As for you, if you walk before Me as your father David walked, with integrity of heart and uprightness, doing everything I have commanded you, and if you keep My statutes and ordinances, I will establish your royal throne over Israel forever, as I promised your father David.

1 Kings 9:4-5 Holman CSB

A HUSBAND'S PRAYER

—

*Dear Lord, help me be a worthy example
to my family members, to my friends,
and to the world. Let the things that I say
and the things that I do show everyone
what it means to be a follower of Your Son.*

Amen

To My Devoted Husband:

Thank You for Your Hard Work

We must do the works of Him who sent Me while it is day. Night is coming when no one can work.

John 9:4 Holman CSB

Making the grade in today's competitive world is not easy. But, even when your workday is long and the workload is difficult, you haven't become discouraged. Thank you for your tireless efforts on behalf of your family.

Thanks for countless sacrifices you've made—you've never stopped giving, and we've never stopped noticing.

If you want to reach your potential,
you need to add a strong work ethic to your talent.

John Maxwell

It may be that the day of judgment will dawn tomorrow; in that case, we shall gladly stop working for a better tomorrow. But not before.

Dietrich Bonhoeffer

The world does not consider labor a blessing, therefore it flees and hates it, but the pious who fear the Lord labor with a ready and cheerful heart, for they know God's command, and they acknowledge His calling.

Martin Luther

Doubtless it is a rule in poetry that if you do your own work well, you will find you have done also work you never dreamed of.

C. S. Lewis

People who work for money only are usually miserable, because there is no fulfillment and no meaning to what they do.

Dave Ramsey

You get the most out of your work when you view yourself as a servant.

Charles Stanley

We are expected to use all available means. We are not allowed to be idle and do nothing simply because we say we are trusting in providence.

C. H. Spurgeon

We must trust as if it all depended on God
and work as if it all depended on us.

C. H. Spurgeon

If, in your working hours, you make the work your end,
you will presently find yourself all unawares inside
the only circle in your profession that really matters.
You will be one of the sound craftsmen,
and other sound craftsmen will know it.

C. S. Lewis

Thank God every morning when you get up that
you have something which must be done,
whether you like it or not. Work breeds a hundred virtues
that idleness never knows.

Charles Kingsley

Whatever you do, do it enthusiastically,
as something done for the Lord and not for men.

Colossians 3:23 Holman CSB

Do not lack diligence; be fervent in spirit; serve the Lord.

Romans 12:11 Holman CSB

He did it with all his heart. So he prospered.

2 Chronicles 31:21 NKJV

Don't work only while being watched, in order to please men,
but as slaves of Christ, do God's will from your heart.
Render service with a good attitude,
as to the Lord and not to men.

Ephesians 6:6-7 Holman CSB

Lazy people's desire for sleep will kill them,
because they refuse to work. All day long they wish for more,
but good people give without holding back.

Proverbs 21:25-26 NKJV

Do not lack diligence; be fervent in spirit; serve the Lord.

Romans 12:11 Holman CSB

And let the beauty of the LORD our God be upon us,
And establish the work of our hands for us;
Yes, establish the work of our hands.

Psalm 90:17 NKJV

A HUSBAND'S PRAYER

—

*Dear Lord, make my work pleasing to You.
Help me to sow the seeds of Your abundance
everywhere I go. Let me be diligent in all
my undertakings and give me the patience
to wait for Your harvest.*

Amen

To My Devoted Husband:

Thank You for

Your

Encouragement

But encourage each other daily, while it is still called today, so that none of you is hardened by sin's deception.

Hebrews 3:13 Holman CSB

When I needed a kind word, you spoke it. When I needed encouragement, you gave it. When I thought that all was lost, you convinced me that it wasn't.

Thank you for being the kind of man who has the confidence to be a source of encouragement to the world and to me.

Zig Ziglar

He climbs highest who helps another up.

People who inspire others are those who see invisible bridges at the end of dead-end streets.

Charles Swindoll

God of our life, there are days when the burdens we carry
chafe our shoulders and weigh us down; when the road
seems dreary and endless, the skies gray and threatening;
when our lives have no music in them, and our hearts are
lonely, and our souls have lost their courage. Flood the path
with light, run our eyes to where the skies are full of promise;
tune our hearts to brave music; give us the sense
of comradeship with heroes and saints of every age;
and so quicken our spirits that we may be able to encourage
the souls of all who journey with us on the road of life,

to Your honor and glory.

St. Augustine

God grant that we may not hinder those who are
battling their way slowly into the light.

Oswald Chambers

To the loved, a word of affection is a morsel,
but to the love-starved, a word of affection can be a feast.

Max Lucado

Words. Do you fully understand their power?
Can any of us really grasp the mighty force behind
the things we say? Do we stop and think before we speak,
considering the potency of the words we utter?

Joni Eareckson Tada

Encouraging others means helping people,
looking for the best in them, and trying to
bring out their positive qualities.

John Maxwell

God is still in the process of dispensing gifts,
and He uses ordinary individuals like us to
develop those gifts in other people.

Howard Hendricks

Make it a rule, and pray to God to help you to keep it,
never to lie down at night without being able to say:
"I have made at least one human being a little wiser,
a little happier, or a little better this day."

Charles Kingsley

In each of my friends there is something that only some
other friend can fully bring out. By myself I am not
large enough to call the whole man into activity;
I want other lights than my own to show all his facets.

C. S. Lewis

Anxiety in a man's heart weighs it down,
but a good word cheers it up.

Proverbs 12:25 Holman CSB

And let us be concerned about one another in order
to promote love and good works.

Hebrews 10:24 Holman CSB

Let the word of Christ dwell in you richly in all wisdom;
teaching and admonishing one another in psalms
and hymns and spiritual songs, singing
with grace in your hearts to the Lord.

Colossians 3:16 KJV

I want their hearts to be encouraged and joined together in love, so that they may have all the riches of assured understanding, and have the knowledge of God's mystery—Christ.

Colossians 2:2 Holman CSB

Carry one another's burdens; in this way you will fulfill the law of Christ.

Galatians 6:2 Holman CSB

Iron sharpens iron, and one man sharpens another.

Proverbs 27:17 Holman CSB

A HUSBAND'S PRAYER

—

*Dear Lord, make me a man who is quick to
celebrate the accomplishments of others.
Make me a source of genuine, lasting
encouragement to my family and friends.
And let my words and deeds be worthy of
Your Son, the One who gives me strength and
salvation, this day and for all eternity.*

Amen

To My Devoted Husband:

Thank You for

Loving

Our Family

Love one another fervently with a pure heart.

1 Peter 1:22 NKJV

No family is perfect, and neither is ours. But even when we've made mistakes, and even when we've been difficult to live with, you've always been there for us. Despite the inevitable challenges of providing for our family, and despite the occasional hurt feelings of family life, you've realized that our clan is God's gift to you. And you've acted accordingly. And we're eternally grateful.

The secret of a happy home life is that the members of the family learn to give and receive love.

Billy Graham

As the first community to which a person is attached
and the first authority under which a person learns to live,
the family establishes society's most basic values.

Charles Colson

God expresses His love by putting us in a family.

Charles Stanley

Never give your family the leftovers and crumbs of your time.

Charles Swindoll

I like to think of my family as a big, beautiful patchwork
quilt—each of us so different yet stitched together
by love and life experiences.

Barbara Johnson

I cannot overemphasize the importance of parental support and love during the formative years of life.

A child's sense of security and well-being is primarily rooted in the stability of his home and family.

James Dobson

You have heard about "quality time" and "quantity time."
Your family needs both.

Jim Gallery

More than any other single factor in a person's formative years, family life forges character.

John Maxwell

There is so much compassion and understanding that is gained when we've experienced God's grace firsthand within our own families.

Lisa Whelchel

A home is a place where we find direction.

Gigi Graham Tchividjian

The Golden Rule begins at home.

Marie T. Freeman

Living life with a consistent spiritual walk deeply influences those we love most.

Vonette Bright

*Love must be without hypocrisy. Detest evil;
cling to what is good. Show family affection to one another with
brotherly love. Outdo one another in showing honor.*

Romans 12:9–10 Holman CSB

*If a kingdom is divided against itself, that kingdom
cannot stand. If a house is divided against itself,
that house cannot stand.*

Mark 3:24–25 Holman CSB

*Now if anyone does not provide for his own relatives,
and especially for his household, he has denied the faith
and is worse than an unbeliever.*

1 Timothy 5:8 Holman CSB

Let them first learn to show piety at home and to repay
their parents; for this is good and acceptable before God.

1 Timothy 5:4 NKJV

Choose for yourselves today the one you will worship . . . .
As for me and my family, we will worship the LORD.

Joshua 24:15 Holman CSB

If they serve Him obediently, they will end their days in
prosperity and their years in happiness.

Job 36:11 Holman CSB

A HUSBAND'S PRAYER

—

Dear Lord, help me to treasure those moments that I spend with my family—and let me demonstrate, through my words and my actions, how much love I feel in my heart for them.

Amen

To My Devoted Husband:

Thank You for

Walking with

Christ

But whoever keeps His word, truly in him the love of God is perfected. This is how we know we are in Him: the one who says he remains in Him should walk just as He walked.

1 John 2:5-6 Holman CSB

By being a godly man and a faithful husband, you have enriched my life, touched my heart, and nourished my soul. By choosing to walk with Jesus, you have given spiritual direction to our family and to me. May God continue to bless you—and us—now and forever, Amen.

—

Teach a man a rule and you help him solve a problem; teach a man to walk with God and you help him solve the rest of his life.

John Eldredge

God's promises aren't celestial life preservers that He throws out to strangers in the storm. They are expressions of His love and care, given to His children who walk with Him and seek to obey Him.

Warren Wiersbe

As a child of God, rest in the knowledge that your Savior precedes you, and He will walk with you through each experience of your life.

Henry Blackaby

I would rather walk with God in the dark than go alone in the light.

Anonymous

A believer comes to Christ; a disciple follows after Him.

Vance Havner

Discipleship means personal, passionate devotion
to a Person, our Lord Jesus Christ.

Oswald Chambers

In our faith we follow in someone's steps.
In our faith we leave footprints to guide others.
It's the principle of discipleship.

Max Lucado

There is no Christianity without a cross, for you cannot be
a disciple of Jesus without taking up your cross.

Henry Blackaby

A follower is never greater than his leader;
a follower never draws attention to himself.

Franklin Graham

Discipleship is a decision to live by what I know about God,
not by what I feel about him or myself or my neighbors.

Eugene Peterson

A disciple is a follower of Christ. That means you take on
His priorities as your own. His agenda becomes your agenda.
His mission becomes your mission.

Charles Stanley

When we truly walk with God throughout our day,
life slowly starts to fall into place.

Bill Hybels

We encouraged, comforted, and implored each one of you to walk worthy of God, who calls you into His own kingdom and glory.

1 Thessalonians 2:12 Holman CSB

The one who loves his life will lose it, and the one who hates his life in this world will keep it for eternal life. If anyone serves Me, he must follow Me. Where I am, there My servant also will be. If anyone serves Me, the Father will honor him.

John 12:25-26 Holman CSB

Follow Me, Jesus told them, "and I will make you into fishers of men!" Immediately they left their nets and followed Him.

Mark 1:17-18 Holman CSB

You did not choose Me, but I chose you. I appointed you that you should go out and produce fruit, and that your fruit should remain, so that whatever you ask the Father in My name, He will give you.

John 15:16 Holman CSB

So you may walk in the way of goodness, and keep to the paths of righteousness. For the upright will dwell in the land, and the blameless will remain in it.

Proverbs 2:20-21 NKJV

For we walk by faith, not by sight.

2 Corinthians 5:7 Holman CSB

A HUSBAND'S PRAYER

—

Dear Lord, each day I will walk with You.
As we walk together, I pray that Your presence
will be reflected in my life, and that
Your love will dwell within my heart
this day and every day.
Amen